WILDLIFE VIEWING AREAS

New England Ecoregions

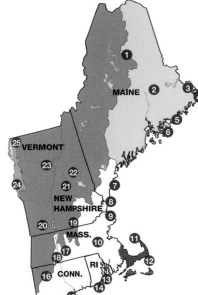

- Eastern Great Lakes Lowlands
- Atlantic Coastal Pine Barrens
- Acadian Plains and Hills
- Northeastern Coastal Zone
- Northeastern Highlands

1. Baxter State Park
2. Sunkhaze Meadows National Wildlife Refuge (NWR)
3. Moosehorn NWR
4. Quoddy Head State Park
5. Petit Manan NWR
6. Acadia National Park
7. Rachel Carson NWR
8. Odiorne Point State Park
9. Parker River NWR
10. Great Meadows NWR
11. Cape Cod National Seashore
12. Monomoy NWR
13. Sachuest Point NWR
14. Ninigret NWR
15. Hammonasset Beach State Park
16. White Memorial Conservation Center
17. Quabbin Reservation – Quabbin Park
18. Arcadia Wildlife Sanctuary
19. Monadnock State Park
20. Green Mountain National Forest
21. Mount Cardigan State Park
22. White Mountain National Forest
23. Groton State Forest
24. Dead Creek Wildlife Management Area
25. Missisquoi NWR

Most illustrations show the adult male in breeding coloration. Colors and markings may be duller or absent during different seasons. The measurements denote the length of species from nose/bill to tail tip. Butterfly measurements denote wingspan. Illustrations are not to scale.

Made in the USA

Waterford Press publishes reference guides that introduce readers to nature observation, outdoor recreation and survival skills. Product information is featured on the website: **www.waterfordpress.com**

 To order or for information on custom published products please call 800-434-2555 or email orderdesk@waterfordpress.com. For permissions or to share comments email editor@waterfordpress.com.

ISBN 978-1-58355-173-8 $7.95 U.S.
9 781583 551738 50795
UPC 8 84682 01055 3
10 9 8 7 6 5 4 3 2 1
2305308

NEW ENGLAND WILDLIFE – A Folding Pocket Guide to Familiar Animals

WATERFORD PRESS

A POCKET NATURALIST® GUIDE

NEW ENGLAND WILDLIFE

A Folding Pocket Guide to Familiar Animals

WATERFORD PRESS

T0123963

SEASHORE LIFE

Spiny Sun Star
Crossaster papposus
To 14 in. (35 cm)

Daisy Brittle Star
Ophiopholis aculeata
To 9 in. (23 cm)

Common Sea Star
Asterias forbesi
To 10 in. (13 cm)
May be tan, brown, orange or olive with orange highlights.

Green Sea Urchin
Strongylocentrotus droebachiensis
To 3 in. (8 cm)

Moon Jellyfish
Aurelia aurita
To 16 in. (40 cm)
Commonly washed up on beaches after storms.

Sand Dollar
Echinarachnius parma
To 3 in. (8 cm)

Sea Gooseberry
Pleurobrachia pileus
To 1 in. (3 cm) wide.

Blue Crab
Callinectes sapidus
To 9 in. (23 cm)

Northern Comb Jelly
Bolinopsis infundibulum
To 6 in. (15 cm)

Fiddler Crab
Uca spp.
To 1.5 in. (4 cm)

Hermit Crab
Pagurus spp.
To 1.25 in. (3.6 cm)
Lives in discarded snail shells.

Green Crab
Carcinus maenas
To 3 in. (8 cm)

Barnacle
Balanus spp. To 3 in. (8 cm)
Often grows in clusters attached to rocks and piers.

Ghost Crab
Ocypode quadrata
To 2 in. (5 cm)

Horseshoe Crab
Limulus polyphemus
To 12 in. (30 cm) wide

Northern Lobster
Homarus americanus
To 3 ft. (90 cm)

INVERTEBRATES

Crane Fly
Tipula spp.
To 2.5 in. (6 cm)

Common Green Darner
Anax junius
To 3 in. (8 cm)
A dragonfly, it rests with its wings held open.

Black-winged Damselfly
Calopteryx maculata
To 1.75 in. (4.5 cm)
Like all damselflies, it rests with its wings held together over its back.

American Cockroach
Periplaneta americana
To 2 in. (5 cm)

Ladybug Beetle
Family Coccinellidae
To .5 in. (1.3 cm)

Firefly
Family Lampyridae
To .75 in. (2 cm)

Bumble Bee
Bombus spp.
To 1 in. (3 cm)
Stout, furry bee is large and noisy.

Viceroy
Limenitis archippus
To 3 in. (8 cm)
Told from similar monarch by its smaller size and the thin, black band on its hindwings.

Paper Wasp
Polistes spp.
To 1 in. (3 cm)
Builds papery hanging nests.

Cabbage White
Pieris rapae
To 2 in. (5 cm)

Eastern Tiger Swallowtail
Pterourus glaucus
To 6 in. (15 cm)

Cloudless Sulphur
Phoebis sennae
To 3 in. (8 cm)

Mourning Cloak
Nymphalis antiopa
To 3.5 in. (9 cm)

Monarch
Danaus plexippus
To 4 in. (10 cm)

Spring Azure
Celastrina ladon
To 1.25 in. (3.2 cm)
One of the earliest spring butterflies.

Red Admiral
Vanessa atalanta
To 2.5 in. (6 cm)

American Copper
Lycaena phlaeas
To 1.25 in. (3.2 cm)

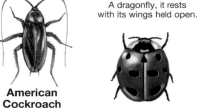

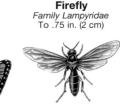

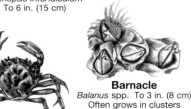

FRESHWATER FISHES

Walleye
Sander vitreus To 40 in. (1 m)

Atlantic Salmon
Salmo salar To 4.5 ft. (1.4 m)

Largemouth Bass
Micropterus salmoides To 40 in. (1 m)
Note prominent side spots.
Jaw joint extends past eye.

Bluegill
Lepomis macrochirus
To 16 in. (40 cm)

Pumpkinseed
Lepomis gibbosus
To 16 in. (40 cm)

Smallmouth Bass
Micropterus dolomieu
To 27 in. (68 cm)
Jaw joint is beneath the eye.

Chain Pickerel
Esox niger To 30 in. (75 cm)
Has chain-like pattern on sides.

Black Crappie
Pomoxis nigromaculatus
To 16 in. (40 cm)

Rainbow Trout
Oncorhynchus mykiss
To 44 in. (1.1 m)

Yellow Perch
Perca flavescens To 16 in. (40 cm)
Has 6-9 dark "saddles" down its side.

Brook Trout
Salvelinus fontinalis To 28 in. (70 cm)
Reddish side spots have blue halos.

Brown Trout
Salmo trutta To 40 in. (1 m)
Has red and black spots on its body.

Lake Trout
Salvelinus namaycush To 4 ft. (1.2 m)
Dark fish is covered in light spots.

Burbot
Lota lota To 3 ft. (90 cm)
Slender fish has a single chin barbel.

Brown Bullhead
Ameiurus nebulosus
To 20 in. (50 cm)
Note prominent whiskers.

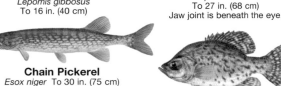

REPTILES & AMPHIBIANS

Eastern Newt
Notophthalmus viridescens
To 6 in. (15 cm)
Immature land form called an eft is red-orange.

Yellow-Spotted Salamander
Ambystoma maculatum
To 10 in. (25 cm)

Bullfrog
Lithobates catesbeianus
To 8 in. (20 cm)
Call is a deep-pitched – *jug-o-rum*.

American Toad
Anaxyrus americanus
To 4.5 in. (11 cm)
Call is a high musical trill lasting up to 30 seconds.

Woodhouse's Toad
Anaxyrus woodhousii
To 5 in. (13 cm)
Call is a sheep-like bleating.

Wood Frog
Lithobates sylvaticus
To 3 in. (8 cm)
Staccato call is duck-like.

Spring Peeper
Pseudacris crucifer
To 1.5 in. (4 cm)
Note dark X on back.
Musical call is a series of short peeps.

Pickerel Frog
Lithobates palustris
To 3.5 in. (9 cm)
Call is a snore-like croak lasting up to 3 seconds.

Painted Turtle
Chrysemys picta To 10 in. (25 cm)

Spotted Turtle
Clemmys guttata To 5 in. (13 cm)

Snapping Turtle
Chelydra serpentina To 18 in. (45 cm)
Note knobby shell and long tail.

Eastern Box Turtle
Terrapene carolina carolina
To 9 in. (23 cm)

Racer
Coluber constrictor To 6 ft. (1.8 m)

Garter Snake
Thamnophis sirtalis To 4 ft. (1.2 m)
Dark snake has yellowish back and side stripes.

Eastern Ribbon Snake
Thamnophis sauritus sauritus
To 40 in. (1 m)
Slender snake has 3 distinct stripes.

Smooth Green Snake
Opheodrys vernalis To 26 in. (65 cm)

Northern Water Snake
Nerodia sipedon To 4.5 ft. (1.4 m)

Copperhead
Agkistrodon contortrix To 52 in. (1.3 m)
Venomous.

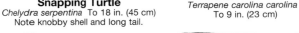

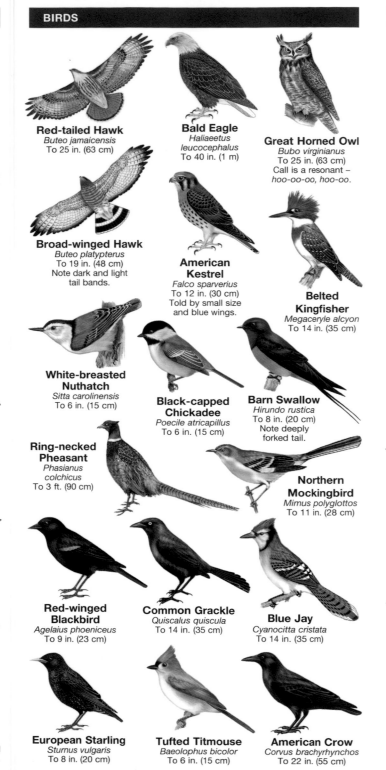

Common Loon
Gavia immer To 3 ft. (90 cm)
Winter / Summer

Pied-billed Grebe
Podilymbus podiceps
To 13 in. (33 cm)
Note banded white bill.

Common Goldeneye
Bucephala clangula To 20 in. (50 cm)

Mallard ♂
Anas platyrhynchos To 28 in. (70 cm)

American Black Duck
Anas rubripes To 25 in. (63 cm)

Wood Duck
Aix sponsa To 20 in. (50 cm)

Great Blue Heron
Ardea herodias To 4.5 ft. (1.4 m)

Great Black-backed Gull
Larus marinus To 32 in. (80 cm)

Ring-billed Gull
Larus delawarensis
To 20 in. (50 cm)
Bill has dark ring.

Canada Goose
Branta canadensis
To 45 in. (1.14 m)

Sanderling
Calidris alba
To 8 in. (20 cm)
Runs in and out
with waves along
shorelines.

Killdeer
Charadrius vociferus
To 12 in. (30 cm)
Note two breast bands.

Double-crested Cormorant
Phalacrocorax auritus
To 3 ft. (90 cm)

Atlantic Puffin
Fratercula arctica
To 12 in. (30 cm)

Northern Gannet
Morus bassanus
To 40 in. (1 m)
Large white sea bird
has black wing tips.

Red-tailed Hawk
Buteo jamaicensis
To 25 in. (63 cm)

Bald Eagle
Haliaeetus leucocephalus
To 40 in. (1 m)

Great Horned Owl
Bubo virginianus
To 25 in. (63 cm)
Call is a resonant –
hoo-oo-oo, hoo-oo.

Broad-winged Hawk
Buteo platypterus
To 19 in. (48 cm)
Note dark and light
tail bands.

American Kestrel
Falco sparverius
To 12 in. (30 cm)
Told by small size
and blue wings.

Belted Kingfisher
Megaceryle alcyon
To 14 in. (35 cm)

White-breasted Nuthatch
Sitta carolinensis
To 6 in. (15 cm)

Black-capped Chickadee
Poecile atricapillus
To 6 in. (15 cm)

Barn Swallow
Hirundo rustica
To 8 in. (20 cm)
Note deeply
forked tail.

Ring-necked Pheasant
Phasianus colchicus
To 3 ft. (90 cm)

Northern Mockingbird
Mimus polyglottos
To 11 in. (28 cm)

Red-winged Blackbird
Agelaius phoeniceus
To 9 in. (23 cm)

Common Grackle
Quiscalus quiscula
To 14 in. (35 cm)

Blue Jay
Cyanocitta cristata
To 14 in. (35 cm)

European Starling
Sturnus vulgaris
To 8 in. (20 cm)

Tufted Titmouse
Baeolophus bicolor
To 6 in. (15 cm)

American Crow
Corvus brachyrhynchos
To 22 in. (55 cm)

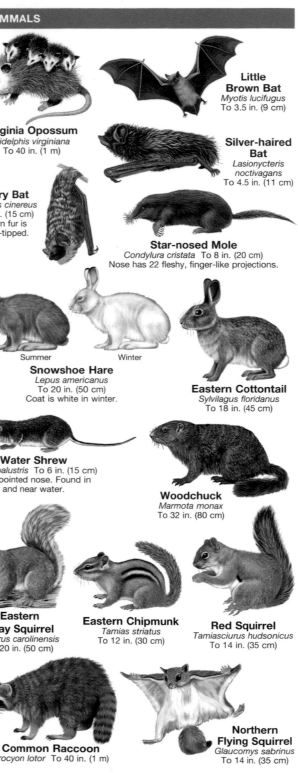

American Robin
Turdus migratorius
To 11 in. (28 cm)

Rock Pigeon
Columba livia
To 13 in. (33 cm)

Mourning Dove
Zenaida macroura
To 13 in. (33 cm)

Eastern Bluebird
Sialia sialis
To 7 in. (18 cm)

Evening Grosbeak
Coccothraustes vespertinus
To 8 in. (20 cm)

Downy Woodpecker
Dryobates pubescens
To 6 in. (15 cm)

Rose-breasted Grosbeak
Pheucticus ludovicianus
To 9 in. (23 cm)

Ruby-throated Hummingbird
Archilochus colubris
To 3.5 in. (9 cm)

Northern Flicker
Colaptes auratus
To 13 in. (33 cm)

American Goldfinch
Spinus tristis
To 5 in. (13 cm)

Eastern Towhee
Pipilo erythrophthalmus
To 9 in. (23 cm)

Cedar Waxwing
Bombycilla cedrorum
To 7 in. (18 cm)

Dark-eyed Junco
Junco hyemalis
To 7 in. (18 cm)

House Sparrow
Passer domesticus
To 6 in. (15 cm)

Northern Cardinal
Cardinalis cardinalis
To 9 in. (23 cm)

House Finch
Haemorhous mexicanus
To 6 in. (15 cm)

Virginia Opossum
Didelphis virginiana
To 40 in. (1 m)

Little Brown Bat
Myotis lucifugus
To 3.5 in. (9 cm)

Hoary Bat
Lasiurus cinereus
To 6 in. (15 cm)
Brown fur is
white-tipped.

Silver-haired Bat
Lasionycteris noctivagans
To 4.5 in. (11 cm)

Star-nosed Mole
Condylura cristata To 8 in. (20 cm)
Nose has 22 fleshy, finger-like projections.

Snowshoe Hare
Lepus americanus
To 20 in. (50 cm)
Coat is white in winter.
Summer / Winter

Eastern Cottontail
Sylvilagus floridanus
To 18 in. (45 cm)

Water Shrew
Sorex palustris To 6 in. (15 cm)
Note pointed nose. Found in
and near water.

Woodchuck
Marmota monax
To 32 in. (80 cm)

Eastern Gray Squirrel
Sciurus carolinensis
To 20 in. (50 cm)

Eastern Chipmunk
Tamias striatus
To 12 in. (30 cm)

Red Squirrel
Tamiasciurus hudsonicus
To 14 in. (35 cm)

Common Raccoon
Procyon lotor To 40 in. (1 m)

Northern Flying Squirrel
Glaucomys sabrinus
To 12 in. (30 cm)

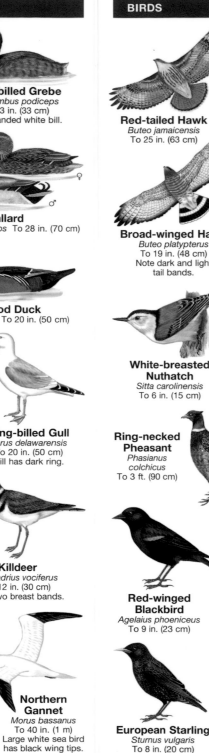

Meadow Vole
Microtus pennsylvanicus
To 7 in. (18 cm)

White-footed Mouse
Peromyscus leucopus To 8 in. (20 cm)

Deer Mouse
Peromyscus maniculatus To 8 in. (20 cm)
Told by white undersides and hairy tail.

Norway Rat
Rattus norvegicus To 18 in. (45 cm)
Brown to gray rodent has a naked tail.

Muskrat
Ondatra zibethicus To 2 ft. (60 cm)
Aquatic rodent.

Common Porcupine
Erethizon dorsatum To 3 ft. (90 cm)
Has coat of long, barbed quills.

American Beaver
Castor canadensis
To 4 ft. (1.2 m)

Northern River Otter
Lontra canadensis
To 52 in. (1.3 m)

Mink
Neovison vison
To 28 in. (70 cm)
Chin is white.

American Marten
Martes americana
To 26 in. (65 cm)

Striped Skunk
Mephitis mephitis
To 32 in. (80 cm)

Long-tailed Weasel
Mustela frenata To 21 in. (53 cm)
Note brown feet.

Short-tailed Weasel
Mustela erminea To 14 in. (35 cm)
Note white feet. Coat may turn
white in winter. Also known as ermine.

Red Fox
Vulpes vulpes To 40 in. (1 m)
Note white-tipped tail.

Common Gray Fox
Urocyon cinereoargenteus
To 3.5 ft. (1.1 m)
Note black-tipped tail.

Bobcat
Lynx rufus To 4 ft. (1.2 m)
Has dark lines on top
of its bobbed tail.

Coyote
Canis latrans To 52 in. (1.3 m)
Note bushy, black-tipped tail.

Moose
Alces alces To 10 ft. (3 m)

White-tailed Deer
Odocoileus virginianus
To 7 ft. (2.1 m)

Harbor Seal
Phoca vitulina
To 6 ft. (1.8 m)

Black Bear
Ursus americanus To 6 ft. (1.8 m)

Gray Seal
Halichoerus grypus
To 8 ft. (2.4 m)

Long-finned Pilot Whale
Globicephala macrorhynchus
To 20 ft. (6 m)

Humpback Whale
Megaptera novaeangliae
To 50 ft. (15 m)

Bottlenosed Dolphin
Tursiops truncatus
To 12 ft. (3.6 m)